To the women in my life. There are too many of you to name (what a blessing), but I hope in reading this, you know I am talking to you. Thank you for loving me and helping to mold me (intentionally or not) into the woman I am today. I am forever grateful for the pieces of yourself that you poured into me. All the best parts of you, I am. Thank you for loving me. **Ma,** thank you for being. Your strength, your love, your will, your dedication, your support has been and will always be unmatched. I am because you are. I am so grateful that you are mine. **Grandma Tina.** If you have left me with a just a small piece of your strength, I know that there is nothing I am incapable of conquering. Thank you for always telling me the truth and never upholding me in my wrongs. I love you and I'll forever miss you. **Dell.** My friend! Your strength inspires me. Motivates me. Your courage gave me the courage to finish this project, embrace the vulnerability, and share this part of me with the world. I love you my friend, and I am so thankful for you. **My sisters.** Thanks for being who I always knew I needed. **My nieces.** Auntie loves you! **Zanae.** You grow girl! I am so proud of you, and so very lucky to be your Godma. I love you. **Ava.** My Lu. I grew because of you. I want to be better, stronger...for you. Thank you for being my mirror and allowing me to view myself through your eyes. You are light. Oh, how I love being your Mama. **My boys.** Not one of you were by chance. You were created and planted not only to remind me of my beauty, but to show me who I can be to this world. Loving the three of you has strengthened me. You saved me. **My husband.** My Rock. For this God designed love. For catching me. For learning who I am. For teaching me. For the way you balance me. For never giving up. Thank you, I prayed for you and I love you.

To those who suffer in silence. All strength is not loud. You don't have to suffer. You are not alone. You matter. You are enough and never too much. Keep going. That amazing thing...yup, the one that scares you...Do it! I am rooting for you. I am you. **This work is dedicated to all of you.**

To the beautiful soul reading this,

Before I go into anything else I would like to first express my gratitude for allowing my gift to become yours. Thank you for investing in me, and in turn investing in you. I pray that this book is received with all the love that went into creating it. It is a work that has inspired me and made me so full during the process.

When I started creating this work of art, I did so because I had a need. I was in a place that I needed to be lifted from. While in that place I sought out things to make me feel better. I stumbled on the magic of making gratitude lists. In my car every morning on my commute to work I would verbally list the things I was grateful for. This changed everything. There was an immediate shift in my life and my attitude. I thought, I should write these down in order to reflect…I have learned I am a memory hoarder (audible laughter). In the midst of wanting to write this down, my "Mom brain" heavily relies on To-Do lists in order to stay organized and productive. I started writing these two lists in the same place, along with my doodles. Jokingly I said, "I should make a Gratitude/To-Do Book!" So, I would have a home for these things. My tribe, instead of laughing, said "you should do this," "There is a need for this!" "Go for it!" To you (you know who you all are), thank you for believing in me. Thank you for pushing me, for being my tribe. I love you! To my husband, thank you for lovingly going along with every idea I sprout. I'm going to say it's because you believe in me, but it may equally be that you want me out your face! (I am chuckling hard right now!) Either way, David, I am grateful for you always saying, "Do it!" I hope you know how much I appreciate you giving me that extra push to do the things I want to do. You're the best and I couldn't be me without you. My children, my unsolicited marketing department…thank you for pushing me, for cheering for me, for believing in me. I love you.

That is how The Give Yourself Grace Journal was born. Along my journey, I picked up other practices, and thought…that could be helpful, I should include that in the book. My hope is that this book will be the reminder for you that it has been for me. A reminder to take care of you. Better yet, I want it to be permission to take care of you first, so that you can continue to pour your magic into those closest to you. You cannot pour from an empty cup. I pray the elements of this book will become tools that will become habits to make you feel better. I created this book with you in mind, and I am so grateful that I could be that vessel. Thanks for being a part of my tribe.

With love and light,

Dei

I believe it is easier to commit to something when you know the benefits. Know that the practices will become much easier as time goes on. It comes back to the old saying "when you know better, you do better.' My prayer is that the components of this book will help you feel better, help keep you grounded, and contribute to your happiness. Remember, this book is about you, and written for you.

Resources required:

- This book
- A pen
- An open heart
- An open mind
- A commitment to yourself

Morning Ritual

A healthy morning routine sets the tone for your day. A great reason to create a morning ritual it is to avoid mental fatigue. Healthy habits and rituals help our lives flow with greater ease and productivity. From experience I know not having a good morning routine and feeling overwhelmed and disorganized were connected. I was being counterproductive. I always say my children do better with routine, but it's all of us, we work better, and it reduces stress and anxiety knowing what our routine looks like each morning. Having the first hour of my day (our day) vary as little as possible with a routine makes me feel powerful. It helps to make me feel in control, non-reactive, reduces anxiety and ensures I'm better equipped and more productive throughout my day.

Gratitude List

Your gratitude list is a thank you to the universe. Two words, "thank you" can be such a healing tool. When I started this practice, I was at one of my lowest life moments. I also thought that there was no way writing down what I was grateful for would change that...boy was I wrong. It can completely shift your mood and attitude. I started by saying the things I was grateful for out loud on my morning commute. The effects were immediate. The universe accepted my thank you, and then gave me more to be grateful for. (I am even grateful for that). Since that point, I have made that a cherished component of my spiritual practice. I have come to realize during times of profound sadness or frustration, expressing my gratitude has made a dramatic impact on my life. The beautiful thing is gratitude cannot inhabit the same emotional space as negativity, it will wash it all those ill feelings away. The gratitude portion of your book will become a bridge to your joy.

To-Do List

Your To-Do lists can be a tool to help your productivity and anxiety. For me, a to-do list is like magic (except you use a pen and paper in lieu waving a magic wand). The days I feel the most productive I have written and followed a to-do list. Being able to check items off my list is a confidence and morale boost. The most invaluable part of the to-do list for me is remembering the things I need to do throughout the day! (I blame it on Mom brain and a combination of my artistry). Additionally, when you write your goals down, it seemingly gives life to them...makes your goal concrete. I can't count the number of times I have had a ton of things to do in my head and then immediately get overwhelmed. After I write a to-do list, I can then focus on one thing at a time. It's pretty amazing how such a simple practice can make you more productive and effective. Keep your to-do list flexible. I don't look at any of my To-Do lists as 'set in stone' because that adds unnecessary stress. Instead use your list as a guide. The purpose of a to-do list is to add structure and help you achieve your goals, not to put pressure on you.

Joy List

Your Joy list contains any and everything that brings joy and makes life authentic. Your joy list is exactly what the name suggests. Write down any and everything that brings you joy. This list serves as a reminder that when times are hard there is something within reach that can change that. This practice will remind you that some of the things that bring the most joy is already in your life or well within reach. Your joy list is never set in stone and you can add to it, if necessary and whenever possible. It's also about making space in your life for the things that bring you joy. When you are intentional and create a space for more joy in your life, you'll also have more inspiration, love and fulfillment. As a mom, a wife, a creative and business owner my joy list is vital! My hope is that your joy list will grow past what these pages can offer.

Self-Care Action Plan

A self-care plan can help you enhance your health/wellbeing and manage your stress. Your body, mind and emotions all give you signs that they are or aren't being taken care of in the way the need to be. Listen to the signs and be mindful. Fill your self-care plan with things that support your wellbeing. Keep your self-plan visible, that will help you commit to the strategies in your plan. Plans can take over a month to become habits, so check-in and be realistic about your own self-care plan. Self-care is the core of our wellbeing. Purposely and actively taking time for yourself to do something that rejuvenates and energizes you is essential. We can take small steps to reduce stress and improve the quality of our lives. Your self-care action plan needs to address all elements of your life. It has been broken down into three categories – physical, mental/emotional & spiritual. Preparing your plan is important; it identifies your goals and the strategies to achieve them. This kind of commitment is only possible when you recognize that your own health and wellbeing are essential, and you acknowledge the importance of honoring yourself and your needs. Take baby steps – don't overwhelm yourself. Give yourself grace.

Self-Check-In

The self-check-in helps develop a habit of acknowledging and nurturing important feelings. After you have made your self-care plan, remember to check-in with yourself. Touching base with yourself daily is a healthy, emotional act. I have learned that when I can be specific and say out loud or write down what is bothering me, I can process that feeling more clearly. By doing this I can gauge if it is worth as much energy as I am putting into the situation. Make space in your life to check in with you daily. Don't be afraid to ask yourself, "How are you?" and then honor your body and emotions taking a moment to care and listen within.

Evening Ritual

Taking time to create rituals that focus on sleep can allow you to fall asleep more easily and sleep more soundly. They also help you wake feeling refreshed and prepared to meet the demands of your day. Try to engage in activities that promote a calming environment, which makes the transition to sleep easier.

Affirmations

Affirmations are positive, specific statements that help you to overcome self-sabotaging and negative thoughts. They help you visualize and believe in what you're affirming to yourself. Affirmations strengthen us first in mind by helping us believe in an action we desire to manifest. Then in body once the thing we have affirmed has manifested. Affirmations should be formed in the present tense, as if they're already happening (i.e. I am, I have). Every affirmation you choose to manifest should be a phrase that's meaningful to you. You need to want this change to happen and it will.

Mood Tracker

In a mood tracker you keep track of how you feel daily. What was your mood; were you happy, tired, stressed or productive? An image of your mood of that month will evolve, and you will end up with a beautiful picture that your moods have created. Focusing on the colors and shapes of lines, will make you feel calm and relaxed. A mood tracker allows you to connect your feelings to what happened during the day. Charting your mood allows you to see patterns in your life. It allows you to better understand your triggers. A benefit of this is that over time you can become more aware of your feelings, and the things that cause them. Take the time to think about you're the moods and colors you want to track and use in your legend.

Love Note to Yourself

Taking just 15 minutes to put some introspective thoughts down on paper is an amazing way to ground. It's important, because dealing with feelings about ourselves, reflecting on how we truly feel, and encouraging ourselves to be kinder and more compassionate can lead to healing, happiness and even better health. Those who wrote about their experiences in letters to themselves felt a sense of relief and helped some understand their emotions and where they came from. More grounded... more positive...more grateful and appreciative. Use these pages to love on yourself. A LOT!

Favorite Quotes

Inspirational quotes can awaken something within us when we read them. They activate our emotions and sometimes when they resonate with us they make us feel better and get our juices, whether creative or critical thinking, flowing. Jot down your favorite quotes on these pages. I live for a good quote!

Vision Board

A vision board is a representation of your desires. Creating a vision board is an exercise in thinking beyond what you believe is possible. They are fun to create and can serve as wonderful tool to motivate and inspire you and push you to manifesting your goals. You can fill your vision board with images and words. This tool allows you to open yourself up to the opportunities to make those thoughts and dreams actually happen over time.

Hand lettered Quotes and Coloring Pages

These pages are my gift to you. I told you I live for a good quote. I have filled these pages with some of my favorite quotes. Quotes that push me, inspire me, remind me of who I am. Some I have illustrated, I hope the love that went into making them is felt and received. Others I have left blank, for you to color in yourself. Coloring is relaxing and may reduce stress, anxiety, depression, and PTSD. I hope these help in lowering your stress, aid in relaxation, and help your boost creativity.

Now that we have gone through each element of the book, let's dive in. Refer to this section whenever you have the need. I am so excited for you to experience this work. I cannot wait to hear what you think about it. I would love to hear your feedback, testimonials, and any remarks. Contact giveyourselfgrace@gmail.com

#GOALS

write them down, make them plain

You are Enough
1/3 Never too
much!

month

Sun	Mon	Tues	Wed	Thu	Fri	Sat

Each day... take a deep breath and start again!

Mood Tracker

MONTH:

make your face key

I feel most safe and loved when...

_____

_____

_____

_____

_____

_____

_____

_____

_____

_____

_____

_____

self ✓ CHECK-IN

LOW moderate HIGH

rate your happiness

WHY DO I FEEL THIS WAY?

_____

_____

_____

_____

my gratitude LIST

_____   _____

_____   _____

_____   _____

_____   _____

_____   _____

_____   _____

_____   _____

_____   _____

_____   _____

_____   _____

The
Universe
WILL RISE
TO
SUPPORT
You

Dear Me,

I am...

beautiful · AMAZING!

LOVED ♡ worthy

confident ♡ HOPEFUL

month

Sun	Mon	Tues	Wed	Thu	Fri	Sat

Each day...
take a deep breath and start again!

Mood Tracker

MONTH:

color key:

☐　　　　☐

☐　☐　☐

I deserve the best in life because...

_____
_____
_____
_____
_____
_____
_____
_____
_____
_____
_____
_____

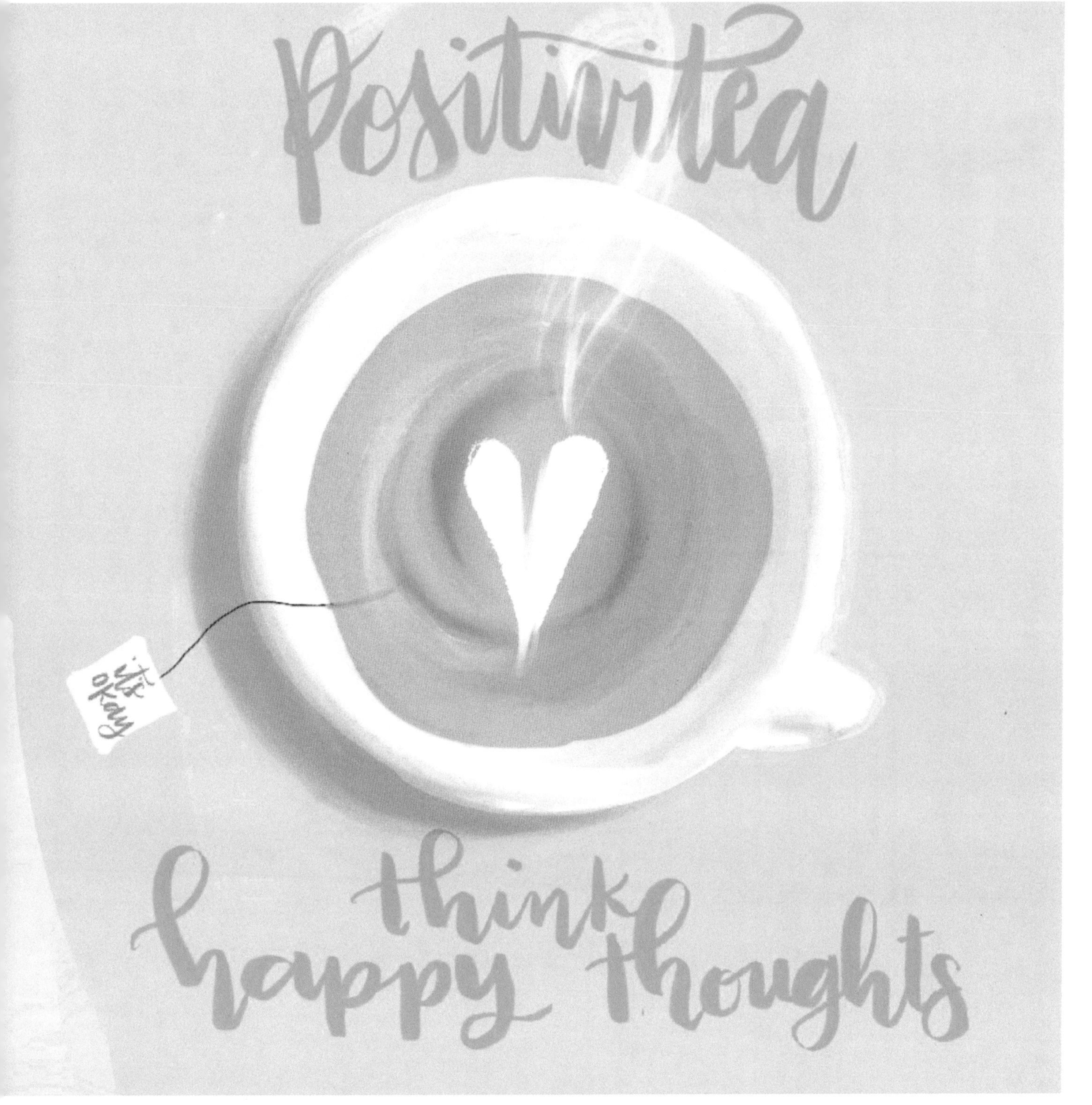
Positivitea
it's okay
think happy thoughts

Dear Me,

month

Sun	Mon	Tues	wed	Thu	Fri	Sat

Each day...
take a deep breath and start again!

Mood Tracker

MONTH:

color key:

I am inspired by...

_____

_____

_____

_____

_____

_____

_____

_____

_____

_____

_____

month

Sun	Mon	Tues	Wed	Thu	Fri	Sat

Each day...
take a deep breath and start again!

mood tracker

MONTH:

color key:

☐ ☐

☐ ☐ ☐

You GROW girl!

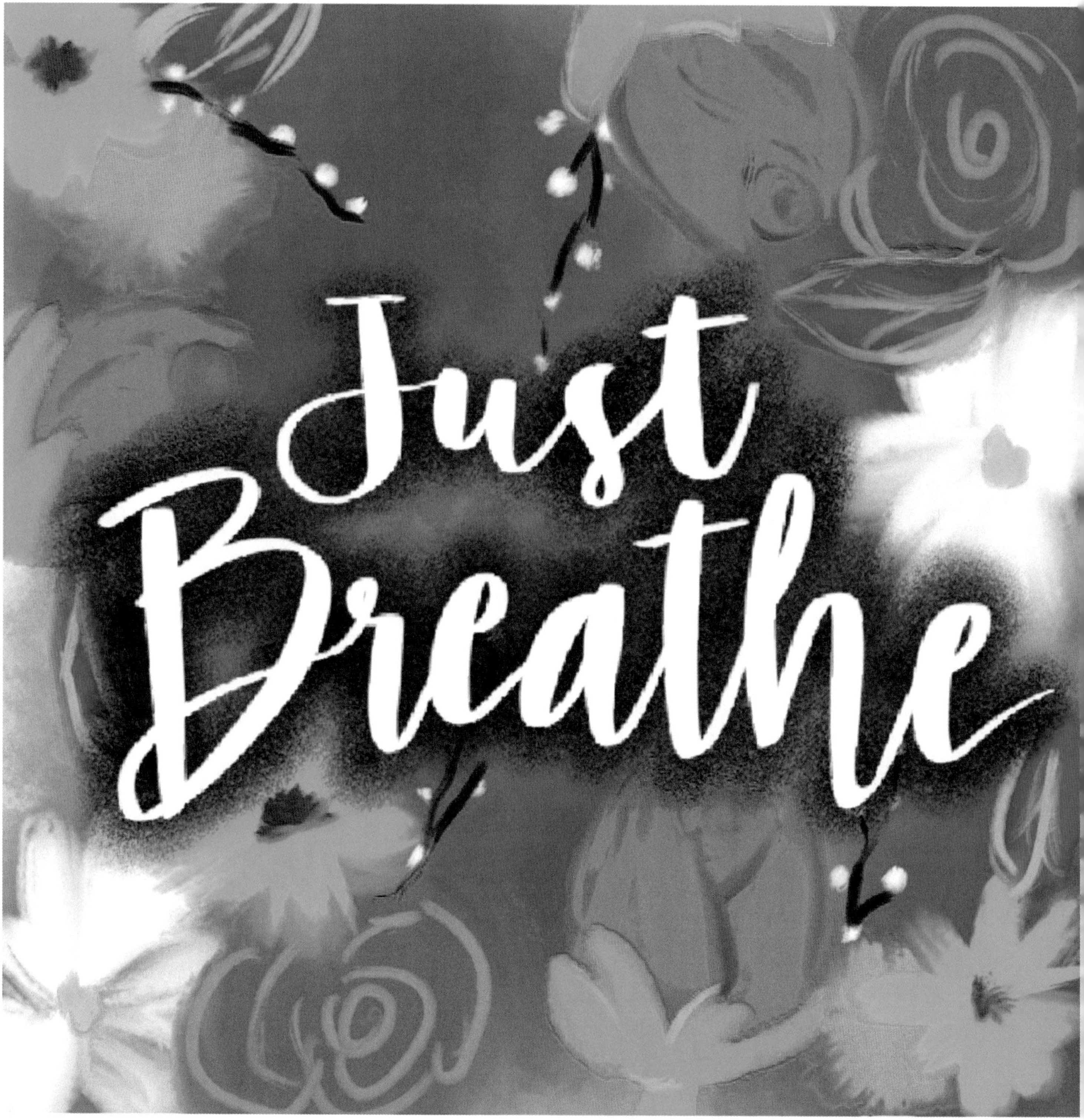
Just
Breathe

I can honor myself by...

_____

_____

_____

_____

_____

_____

_____

_____

_____

_____

_____

Things that make me Smile

Water Yourself

month

Sun	Mon	Tues	Wed	Thu	Fri	Sat

Each day...
take a deep breath and start
again!

mood tracker

MONTH:

☐   color key: ☐

☐   ☐   ☐

Courage tastes like...

_____

_____

_____

_____

_____

_____

_____

_____

_____

_____

_____

_____

month

Sun	Mon	Tues	Wed	Thu	Fri	Sat

Each day...
take a deep breath and start again!

Dear Me,

my FAVORITE
Quotes

to-Do list

month

Sun	Mon	Tues	wed	Thu	Fri	Sat

Each day...
take a deep breath and start
again!

Mood Tracker

MONTH:

color key:

Nobody knows that I...

_____

_____

_____

_____

_____

_____

_____

_____

_____

_____

_____

month

Sun	Mon	Tues	wed	Thu	Fri	Sat

Each day...
take a deep breath and start again!

Mood TRACKER

MONTH:

color key:

THE BEST DAY EVER LOOKS LIKE...

now make it happen!

Grow through what you go through

Sun	Mon	Tues	Wed	Thu	Fri	Sat

month

Each day...
take a deep breath and start again!

mood tracker

MONTH:

color key:

Love smells like...

_____

_____

_____

_____

_____

_____

_____

_____

_____

_____

_____

_____

Find your
TRIBE
love them
HARD

to-Do list

month

Sun	Mon	Tues	Wed	Thu	Fri	Sat

Each day...
take a deep breath and start again!

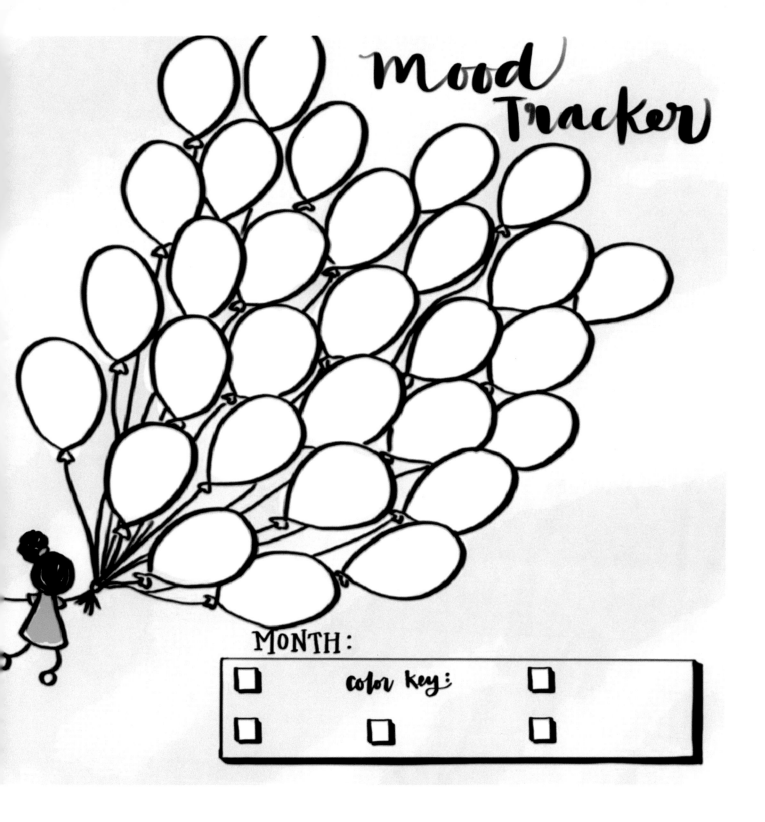

Mood Tracker

MONTH:

color key:

Letting go looks like...

_____

_____

_____

_____

_____

_____

_____

_____

_____

_____

_____

Dear Me,

what I love most about me...

month

Sun	Mon	Tues	Wed	Thu	Fri	Sat

Each day...
take a deep breath and start again!

MOOD

good vibes only

MONTH:

color key:

I need to forgive myself for...

_____

_____

_____

_____

_____

_____

_____

_____

_____

_____

_____

_____

SHE HAS *fire* IN HER *soul* & *grace* IN HER *heart*

month

Sun	Mon	Tues	Wed	Thu	Fri	Sat

Each day...
take a deep breath and start again!

Mood Tracker

MONTH:

color key:

The best lessons I have learned are...

self ✓ CHECK-IN

LOW

moderate

HIGH

rate your happiness

WHY DO I FEEL THIS WAY?

_____

_____

_____

_____

Morning Ritual

Evening Ritual

my gratitude LIST

_____   _____

_____   _____

_____   _____

_____   _____

_____   _____

_____   _____

_____   _____

_____   _____

_____   _____

_____   _____

I knew I was strong when...

_____

_____

_____

_____

_____

_____

_____

_____

_____

_____

_____

You're always had the power my dear you just had to learn it for yourself

-The Wizard of Oz

I am...

beautiful · AMAZING!

LOVED ♡ worthy

confident ♡ HOPEFUL

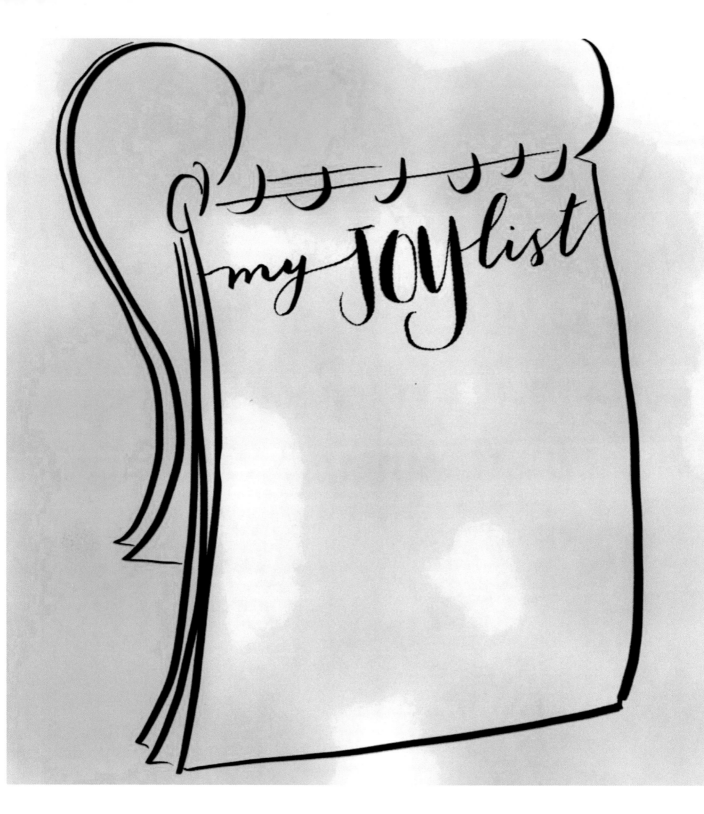

focus ON THE LIGHT

Notes

Notes

Notes

Notes

Notes

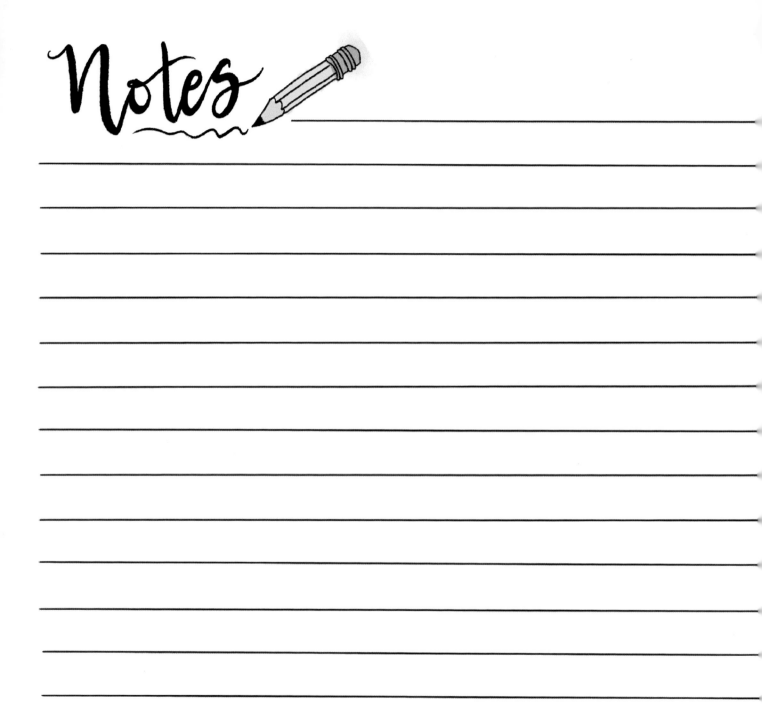

Notes